What You Need to Succeed

Instructions to get you going

This link will get you started, guiding you through all the science and steps designed into this planner. Click the QR code or type in: BIGGrowthPlanner.info.

Tools to keep your momentum

GrowBIG AI is your gratis, on-call AI thought partner. Get help to prioritize actions, deepen relationships, and accelerate opportunities. Sign up for free at GrowBIG.ai.

Give to Grow provides a broad overview of how to grow a book of business. Buy it wherever books are sold. Also, get a free training course on the book's content at GiveToGrow.info.

GrowBIG Training and Coaching gives you a fast path to success. Bring us in to train your team or get 1:1 support. To learn more, visit BunnellIdeaGroup.com or email contact@bunnellideagroup.com.

Plan: Prioritize Your Quarter

1 Conduct a Self-Assessment

2 Cut to Climb

3 Prioritize Your Top Insights

4 Define This Quarter's Wins

Conduct a Self-Assessment

The best place to start is with a self-assessment. Think about this self-assessment like scores for artistic events in the Olympics, like platform diving or gymnastics floor routines. They're not perfect, but they give a numerical score for an abstract skill. This exercise will give you a score for the robustness of your Business Development (BD) platform and habits.

Fill out the following questions using the definitions below. Important: Note that the scale doubles for the Consistency questions. That's because staying consistent in your BD efforts is the most important area to focus on. So in that section, you can get up to 10 points per question. What's a 5 in the other sections is a 10 in Consistency, what was a 4 becomes an 8 and so on.

Use this scale:

1   I could use a few pointers here.
2   I'm doing OK on this.
3   Ah! One of my strengths.
4   I am exceptionally good at this.
5   I know this topic well enough that I'm frequently asked to mentor or coach others on it.

Vision

Question	Score (1 to 5)
Have I defined the areas where my ideal clients will be spending money on services like mine in the future? Do I know where the trend in spend is going?	
Do I have a clear brand I promote internally and externally that is aligned with these areas?	
Do I have a clear BD strategy for each step in the process, from generating leads to closing deals, and do I follow it consistently?	
Do I have a vision for integrating colleagues, prospects, clients, and others I partner with in my overall business strategy?	
Total Vision Score (Max = 20)	

Relationship

Question	Score (1 to 5)
Have I identified—and written down—the key characteristics of my ideal clients?	
Have I used these key characteristics to identify the exact people internally and externally that I'd like to get introduced to and invest in, and have I written down those names?	
Do I have a method for investing in and being helpful to this list of most important people?	
Do I have an appropriate number of touchpoints to stay top of mind with these most important people, and do I track my touchpoints?	
Total Relationship Score (Max = 20)	

Measurement

Question	Score (1 to 5)
How much new work did I generate (or play a significant role in generating) in the last quarter compared with how much I would have liked to?	
How much time did I dedicate to BD in the last quarter compared to how much I would have liked to?	
Do I have a system for measuring the leading and lagging measures of my personal BD success?	
Do I have a system for measuring the leading and lagging measures of my team's BD success?	
Total Measurement Score (Max = 20)	

Consistency

Question	Score (1 to 10)*
Do I have an ongoing *series of meetings* to manage my BD like a project that I was hired to lead, including tracking progress and planning my next actions?	
Do I have an *easy-to-use documentation system* to manage BD actions and steps to the level I would for managing an important project I'm paid to lead?	
Do I hold myself accountable for my BD commitments?	
Do I celebrate my incremental BD successes (not just the end goal of closing business deals but also the progress toward that end) personally and with my colleagues?	
Total Consistency Score (Max = 40)	

**Grand Total
(Max 100)**

* Remember that the Consistency questions are graded on a 1 to 10 scale, not 1 to 5.

Cut to Climb

Identify the least valuable 50 hours you spent in the last quarter, then decide how you can eliminate, delegate, or automate these tasks so that you can focus that time on more valuable BD activities. See the detailed instructions at BIGGrowthPlanner.info for more on how to do this. There's also much more in the "Succeed in the Long Term" chapter of *Give to Grow*.

Activity to eliminate, delegate, or automate:	Hours saved per activity:

Grand Total Hours Saved

Top Insights

Review your Self-Assessment and Cut to Climb results.
What are the most important things you want to change?

Now look forward. What do you want to make sure you focus
on in the next quarter?

Define This Quarter's Wins

Define this quarter's wins and how you'll know each is done. They can be external or internal, a hard metric focus or just a feeling. Choose whatever works for this quarter—the key is writing the goals down.

I want to accomplish...   **I'll know it's done when...**

The growth habit or skill I'd like to focus on this quarter is...

I'll incorporate my team and colleagues into my plan by…

I'll celebrate my success by doing something just for me when I hit my goals. This quarter I will…

Act: Build Momentum Each Week

Week 1 | Plan Week of ________________________

☐ **I've reviewed and updated my Opportunity and Protemoi Lists.**

☐ **I've reviewed my quarterly goals.**

Most Important Things

☐ **1**

☐ **2**

☐ **3**

Habits and Skills Development: I can practice my focused habit or skill this week by…

Leverage 34x Access

Meeting	Request or Recommendation

☐ **I've added any needed reminders and entries to my upcoming week's calendar.**

Week 1 | Reflect

Measurement

Number of MITs completed:	Business Development hours:	Did I do all I could to focus on growth?
		☐ Yes ☐ No

The #1 thing I learned this week is...

I put myself in a better position to win work in the future because I...

Week 2 | Plan   Week of ______________________

☐ I've reviewed and updated my Opportunity and Protemoi Lists.

☐ I've reviewed my quarterly goals.

Most Important Things

☐ 1

☐ 2

☐ 3

Habits and Skills Development: I can practice my focused habit or skill this week by...

Leverage 34x Access

Meeting	**Request or Recommendation**

☐ I've added any needed reminders and entries to my upcoming week's calendar.

Week 2 | Reflect

Measurement

**Number
of MITs
completed:**

**Business
Development
hours:**

**Did I do all
I could to focus
on growth?**

☐ Yes

☐ No

The #1 thing I learned this week is...

**I put myself in a better position to win work in the future
because I...**

Week 3 | Plan   Week of ______________________

☐ I've reviewed and updated my Opportunity and Protemoi Lists.

☐ I've reviewed my quarterly goals.

Most Important Things

☐ 1

☐ 2

☐ 3

Habits and Skills Development: I can practice my focused habit or skill this week by...

Leverage 34x Access

Meeting	Request or Recommendation

☐ I've added any needed reminders and entries to my upcoming week's calendar.

Week 3 | Reflect

Measurement

Number of MITs completed:	Business Development hours:	Did I do all I could to focus on growth?
		☐ Yes ☐ No

The #1 thing I learned this week is...

I put myself in a better position to win work in the future because I...

Week 4 | Plan   Week of _______________

☐ **I've reviewed and updated my Opportunity and Protemoi Lists.**

☐ **I've reviewed my quarterly goals.**

Most Important Things

☐ 1

☐ 2

☐ 3

Habits and Skills Development: I can practice my focused habit or skill this week by...

Leverage 34x Access

Meeting	Request or Recommendation

☐ **I've added any needed reminders and entries to my upcoming week's calendar.**

Week 4 | Reflect

Measurement

Number of MITs completed:	Business Development hours:	Did I do all I could to focus on growth?
		☐ Yes
		☐ No

The #1 thing I learned this week is...

I put myself in a better position to win work in the future because I...

Week 5 | Plan Week of _______________________

☐ **I've reviewed and updated my Opportunity and Protemoi Lists.**

☐ **I've reviewed my quarterly goals.**

Most Important Things

☐ 1

☐ 2

☐ 3

Habits and Skills Development: I can practice my focused habit or skill this week by...

Leverage 34x Access

Meeting	Request or Recommendation

☐ **I've added any needed reminders and entries to my upcoming week's calendar.**

Week 5 | Reflect

Measurement

Number of MITs completed:	Business Development hours:	Did I do all I could to focus on growth?
		☐ Yes ☐ No

The #1 thing I learned this week is...

I put myself in a better position to win work in the future because I...

Week 6 | Plan   Week of ______________________

☐ **I've reviewed and updated my Opportunity and Protemoi Lists.**

☐ **I've reviewed my quarterly goals.**

Most Important Things

☐ 1

☐ 2

☐ 3

Habits and Skills Development: I can practice my focused habit or skill this week by...

Leverage 34x Access

Meeting	Request or Recommendation

☐ **I've added any needed reminders and entries to my upcoming week's calendar.**

Week 6 | Reflect

Measurement

Number of MITs completed:	**Business Development hours:**	**Did I do all I could to focus on growth?**
		☐ Yes
		☐ No

The #1 thing I learned this week is...

I put myself in a better position to win work in the future because I...

Week 7 | Plan   Week of _______________

☐ **I've reviewed and updated my Opportunity and Protemoi Lists.**

☐ **I've reviewed my quarterly goals.**

Most Important Things

☐ 1

☐ 2

☐ 3

Habits and Skills Development: I can practice my focused habit or skill this week by...

Leverage 34x Access

Meeting	Request or Recommendation

☐ **I've added any needed reminders and entries to my upcoming week's calendar.**

Week 7 | Reflect

Measurement

Number of MITs completed:	**Business Development hours:**	**Did I do all I could to focus on growth?**
		☐ Yes
		☐ No

The #1 thing I learned this week is...

I put myself in a better position to win work in the future because I...

Week 8 | Plan — Week of _______________________

☐ I've reviewed and updated my Opportunity and Protemoi Lists.

☐ I've reviewed my quarterly goals.

Most Important Things

☐ 1

☐ 2

☐ 3

Habits and Skills Development: I can practice my focused habit or skill this week by...

Leverage 34x Access

Meeting	Request or Recommendation

☐ I've added any needed reminders and entries to my upcoming week's calendar.

Week 8 | Reflect

Measurement

Number of MITs completed:	Business Development hours:	Did I do all I could to focus on growth?
		☐ Yes
		☐ No

The #1 thing I learned this week is...

I put myself in a better position to win work in the future because I...

Week 9 | Plan Week of _______________________

☐ I've reviewed and updated my Opportunity and Protemoi Lists.

☐ I've reviewed my quarterly goals.

Most Important Things

☐ 1

☐ 2

☐ 3

Habits and Skills Development: I can practice my focused habit or skill this week by...

Leverage 34x Access

Meeting	Request or Recommendation

☐ I've added any needed reminders and entries to my upcoming week's calendar.

Week 9 | Reflect

Measurement

Number of MITs completed:	Business Development hours:	Did I do all I could to focus on growth?
		☐ Yes ☐ No

The #1 thing I learned this week is...

I put myself in a better position to win work in the future because I...

Week 10 | Plan Week of ______________________

☐ I've reviewed and updated my Opportunity and Protemoi Lists.

☐ I've reviewed my quarterly goals.

Most Important Things

☐ 1

☐ 2

☐ 3

Habits and Skills Development: I can practice my focused habit or skill this week by...

Leverage 34x Access

Meeting   **Request or Recommendation**

☐ I've added any needed reminders and entries to my upcoming week's calendar.

Week 10 | Reflect

Measurement

Number of MITs completed:	Business Development hours:	Did I do all I could to focus on growth?
		☐ Yes ☐ No

The #1 thing I learned this week is...

I put myself in a better position to win work in the future because I...

Week 11 | Plan   Week of _______________

☐ I've reviewed and updated my Opportunity and Protemoi Lists.

☐ I've reviewed my quarterly goals.

Most Important Things

☐ 1

☐ 2

☐ 3

Habits and Skills Development: I can practice my focused habit or skill this week by...

Leverage 34x Access

Meeting	Request or Recommendation

☐ I've added any needed reminders and entries to my upcoming week's calendar.

Week 11 | Reflect

Measurement

Number of MITs completed:	Business Development hours:	Did I do all I could to focus on growth?
		☐ Yes
		☐ No

The #1 thing I learned this week is…

I put myself in a better position to win work in the future because I…

Week 12 | Plan Week of ________________________

☐ I've reviewed and updated my Opportunity and Protemoi Lists.

☐ I've reviewed my quarterly goals.

Most Important Things

☐ 1

☐ 2

☐ 3

Habits and Skills Development: I can practice my focused habit or skill this week by…

Leverage 34x Access

Meeting	Request or Recommendation

☐ I've added any needed reminders and entries to my upcoming week's calendar.

Week 12 | Reflect

Measurement

Number of MITs completed:

Business Development hours:

Did I do all I could to focus on growth?

☐ Yes

☐ No

The #1 thing I learned this week is...

I put myself in a better position to win work in the future because I...

Week 13 | Plan Week of _______________

☐ I've reviewed and updated my Opportunity and Protemoi Lists.

☐ I've reviewed my quarterly goals.

Most Important Things

☐ 1

☐ 2

☐ 3

Habits and Skills Development: I can practice my focused habit or skill this week by...

Leverage 34x Access

Meeting	Request or Recommendation

☐ I've added any needed reminders and entries to my upcoming week's calendar.

Week 13 | Reflect

Measurement

**Number
of MITs
completed:**

**Business
Development
hours:**

**Did I do all
I could to focus
on growth?**

☐ Yes

☐ No

The #1 thing I learned this week is...

**I put myself in a better position to win work in the future
because I...**

Quarterly Reflection: Look Back To Learn

Looking Back

How I feel about my accomplishments:

How I improved the habit or skill I focused on:

MITs Success Rate

$$\frac{\text{done}}{\text{attempted}} = \quad \%$$

Business Development Hours

$$\frac{\text{actual}}{\text{goal}} = \quad \%$$

Looking Forward

The #1 thing I would change is...

The #1 thing I need to keep doing is...

I am particularly proud that...

The specific thing I did that I'm proud of is...

And the reason that action is so satisfying is because...

About Bunnell Idea Group (BIG)

BIG was born in a moment of fear.

Our founder, Mo Bunnell, had just passed all the actuarial exams to reach the highest designation, Fellow of the Society of Actuaries. Mo and his firm orchestrated a role change—Mo went from being rewarded as an expert to one focused on Business Development (BD) with some of the largest clients at his firm. In general terms, Mo's responsibilities went from senior associate to senior partner in a day, skipping the partner role altogether.

That's when the fear kicked in.

Mo realized there was no "manual" for BD. Success in his new role meant he had to get great at BD, and fast. Why did clients say yes to some offers and not others? How are deep, trusting relationships formed? How can we stay on top of BD, even when we're busy?

Over years of painstaking research and trial and error, the beginnings of a system emerged. Before this system, Mo worked insane hours, got moderate results, and was exhausted. After this system, Mo worked reasonable hours, got some of the best results across his entire world-wide organization, and thrived on helping his clients succeed.

You can have a system too, and this planner will help you implement it.

If you want a high-level overview of how to grow, read our books *Give to Grow* and *The Snowball System*. For a 24/7 thought partner on the next move to make, sign up for our free AI tool at GrowBIG.ai.

And, if you want deeper support, check out our training and coaching services at BunnellIdeaGroup.com.

We love helping people win the work they want with the clients they want. We've trained and coached tens of thousands of high-end professionals, and we'd love to help you too.

If we can help you think through anything from a specific issue to a large-scale initiative, just email us at contact@bunnellideagroup.com.

My Opportunities

Opportunity	Next step

Protemoi and Opportun

My Protemoi People

Name	Next step